Here is a clear, concise guide to writing
research and term papers. Every step—from
selecting the topic to typing the final draft—is
simply but thoroughly explained. Students will find
WRITING THE RESEARCH AND TERM PAPER
of invaluable assistance in the achievement
of improved grades and better learning.

P9-AOX-719

Travis Hauser is Chairman of the English Department
at Geneva High School in New York. The author
of several books on English he also conducts the weekly
syndicated newspaper column, "Problems of Education."
Lee Learner Gray, formerly an assistant editor for
Scholastic Magazines, is the author of **Better and
Faster Reading** and **How We Choose a President**.

WRITING THE RESEARCH
AND TERM PAPER

TRAVIS L. HAUSER and LEE LEARNER GRAY

LAUREL-LEAF BOOKS

Published by Dell Publishing Co., Inc.
1 Dag Hammarskjold Plaza
New York, N.Y. 10017

Copyright © 1964 by Cambridge Book Company, Inc.
Laurel-Leaf Library ® TM 766734, Dell Publishing Co., Inc.

ISBN: 0-440-99705-4

Reprinted by arrangement with Cambridge Book
Company, Inc., Bronxville, N.Y.

Printed in U.S.A.

First Dell Printing—November 1965
Twenty-first Dell Printing—August 1984

Book Club Edition

TABLE OF CONTENTS

PREFACE

Writing the Research and Term Paper has been prepared in answer to innumerable requests from students and teachers for a clear, concise explanation of the technique of writing a research report. There is a definite pattern of thought and of work that must be followed in order to make such a report successful. The very nature of the serious research that precedes the writing of the paper means that logical steps must be followed, one after the other.

Unlike an essay or a short composition, a research paper is the result of locating and studying factual material that other people have written. The collection of this material, the digestion, arrangement and interpretation of it make up the preparation of a research report.

Writing the Research and Term Paper gives the step-by-step procedure. It goes farther than that, with tips on fast reading, on clear note-taking, on library techniques, and even on typing the final draft. These tips will make certain phases of the research much easier, and will make the final copy not only more readable, but more attractive.

It is our hope that this pamphlet will take some of the unfounded mystery out of preparing the research report. We hope also that it will help students avoid the stage-fright that often besets them at the thought of tackling such an assignment.

— THE AUTHORS

PART I
THE MECHANICS OF THE RESEARCH PAPER

1. WHAT IS A RESEARCH PAPER?

Your research paper is your factual presentation of other people's findings on a given subject. Its purpose is twofold: (1) to provide others with an organized, thorough summary of information on your subject; (2) to help you master the basic techniques of scholarship. By doing a research paper you will learn where and how to locate information quickly; how to use your library; how to take fast, accurate notes; how to make footnotes and bibliographies so others can use your sources and, most important, how to organize your thoughts.

A good research paper, therefore, contains more facts than opinions, and the opinions it *does* contain are the opinions of your *sources*, not yours. If properly done, however, your research paper should still be original; for the way in which you present the material and your choice of what to use and what not to use in your report will indicate what you think are the most important or unimportant aspects of your topic. Often, too, you can show how two different sources, though they seem to disagree, are really saying the same thing in a different way. This is the research paper at its best—helpful not only to you in organizing your thoughts but helpful to others in seeing new connections between familiar facts.

2. PLANNING YOUR RESEARCH PAPER

Do you squirm at the very thought of planning and writing a research paper? Do you balk mentally at the idea of having to wade through miles of books and acres of words to find the material you will need?

If the prospect does not please you it is undoubtedly because in the past you went about writing a serious report inefficiently and unwisely. You probably were burdened with a subject that did not really and truly interest you. You may have kept putting off the job until the nearness of your deadline threw you into a panic.

When your teacher assigns a research paper, you are expected to work on it over a period of time. It may take many weeks, perhaps even several months, to find and organize all the material you will need for an accurate, interesting report of even 1000 to 2000 words. The report will be assigned far enough in advance of the deadline to give you the necessary time.

You should take advantage of this by getting to work on your report at once. If you put it off until later you will miss the pleasure of slowly and carefully digging up facts. You'll miss the fun of the treasure hunt. Your final report, unfortunately, will reveal all too clearly that you hurried. Awkward organization and careless writing will give you away.

There is nothing mysterious or frightening about planning a long report. There are definite steps to follow:

1. Decide on a topic.
2. Plan a rough outline of your research or term paper.
3. Round up all available research sources.
4. Read helpful source material, and take clear, accurate notes.
5. Revise your original outline.
6. Write your first draft.
7. Revise your first draft.
8. Organize footnotes, bibliography and other mechanical sections.
9. Prepare your final report.

These steps never change. Whatever the topic, or whoever gives the assignment, the steps are always the same. You will follow them in high school, in college, and during your business career. You will follow them as an adult member of various organizations. So master these steps now.

3. CHOOSING YOUR TOPIC

You may have no choice in the matter of the subject of your report. The subject will be assigned to you, and you'll be required to complete it on time.

Your science teacher might, for instance, assign the topic "Tsutsugamushi Disease." Though you may never have heard of it before, finding out what it is all about can be a real adventure.

In assigning a research report, your teacher may make some general suggestions about subjects you might choose, and leave the final choice up to you. Since you are going to live with your report for some time, you owe it to yourself to choose a topic in which you are genuinely interested. It might be a subject you already know a little about, but would like to know more. It might be something brand new which arouses your curiosity.

Your English teacher will probably agree to any topic that lends itself to research. Your social studies or science teacher will expect you to confine yourself to a subject in that field. Your teacher will gladly confer with you about your choice of a topic that fits the assignment and that really interests you.

Your teacher's suggestions will undoubtedly be general in nature. You will want to narrow down such general ideas to a specific topic. Discuss your choice with your teacher. Once you have started to work on a topic, it might prove difficult to switch to another if your teacher does not approve of it.

Be careful to choose a subject that you can handle thoroughly in the number of words expected of you. "Jazz," for instance, would be impossibly big. It could be narrowed down to "The Beginnings of Jazz in New Orleans."

Be careful, too, in narrowing your subject, not to back yourself into a corner. It is possible to limit your subject so rigidly that you cannot find enough material for your report. "The Nesting Habits of the Black-Necked Swan" might appeal to you as a possible topic, but your local library might not provide enough facts for you to use. Broadening the topic to include the nesting habits of various kinds of swans might give you more possible research sources.

A good way to narrow a large subject and thus come to a decision on your topic is to get a bird's-eye view of it in an encyclopedia. Look up the subject that interests you most and skim quickly through the encyclopedia article. See how wide a field it covers. Read the cross-references to other articles. Are there many, or few? If the subject looks too big or too limited, read up on your second choice of subject. Only after a preliminary search for information on your topic choice should you decide whether or not it is the topic for you to write about.

4. MAKING A ROUGH OUTLINE

Your bird's-eye view of your chosen topic will give you an idea of how much there is to learn about it. If you already knew all there was to know you would not have to do any research. But, since you do not yet know all the facts, you cannot yet outline your report finally and definitely.

Your rough outline should be a list of the various angles you want to investigate. It might be a list of questions to which you want to find the answers. Your rough outline will help you to stick to your subject as you do your research.

The outline can be in any form that would be most helpful

to you. It might be the formal I., II., III., IV. outline in topic or sentence form.

Electing a President

I. Political parties.
II. Nominating conventions.
III. Election machinery.
IV. The Campaign.
V. Electoral college.
VI. Election day.

How to Take Good Pictures

I. Reasons for taking pictures.
II. The necessary equipment.
III. Composing the picture.
IV. Lighting.
V. Miscellaneous suggestions.

Each one of these headings may be divided into at least two smaller parts. For example, III might be divided as follows:

III. Composing the picture.
    A. One main point of interest.
    B. Attractive material.
    C. Simple background.
        1. No electric wires.
        2. No picket fences.

Keep your rough outline very simple. After all, it is just a skeleton of your final report. As you do your research you will dig up facts or interesting material that will fit into one place or another of this rough framework. You may, on the other hand, find no suitable material that will round out a subtopic. You may, in the end, strike the subtopic from your final outline, or you may decide to research further.

On page 31 you will see how a rough outline looks in final, revised form. The reading will be done, the material assembled, and the topics and subtopics arranged in order.

5. ROUNDING UP YOUR RESEARCH SOURCES

Your library will probably be your first research stop. Does the sight of all the books you might wade through overwhelm you? If you're an old hand at using your library you'll know exactly where and how to search for the material you need. You'll know what your library has to offer, how to find what you want, and how to use it after you've found it. But if you're a library-dawdler, you will probably stare vacantly at bookshelves, flip idly through many useless volumes, wander around vaguely, and end up putting your problem to the librarian.

She will undoubtedly steer you into the reference room (where you could have gone all by yourself) for a good look at the general reference material your library has to offer. Dictionaries, encyclopedias, atlases and other helpful reference books are usually kept on open shelves where you can consult them freely. These books cannot be taken from the library, so you must do your reading there.

A. Encyclopedias

Begin your research by looking up your topic in the encyclopedia in which you first had a bird's-eye view. Read the basic reference and all cross references very carefully. Search for your topic in every encyclopedia your library owns. They provide an easy source for background material and a quick reference for facts. Some of the most widely used encyclopedias are:

(1) *Encyclopaedia Britannica*. This is the most scholarly encyclopedia. 24 volumes of long articles written and signed by specialists. The *Britannica Book of the Year* is the annual supplement.

(2) *Encyclopedia Americana*. The *Americana* is a good general encyclopedia, especially strong in the fields of science, technology, government and business. 30 volumes, and annual yearbook.

(3) *Collier's Encyclopedia.* General encyclopedia, for laymen; emphasizes modern Western World; strong in contemporary science and biography. 20 volumes; annual yearbook.

(4) *New International Encyclopedia.* This set of 25 volumes covers many very small subjects, including titles of famous works of literature and names of fictitious characters. A yearbook is published annually.

(5) *Columbia Encyclopedia, Columbia-Viking Encyclopedias, Lincoln Library of Essential Information.* One-volume encyclopedias that give brief accounts of a subject.

Nearly every encyclopedia has an index, usually found in the last volume. It often gives additional page references where your subject is mentioned under other topics.

B. Biographical Dictionaries

Encyclopedias are not the only quick source of material on your subject, however. Your library will have biographical dictionaries such as:

(1) *Who's Who in America.* Prominent living Americans; 1899 to date; biennial.

(2) *Who Was Who in America.* Americans no longer living.

(3) *Dictionary of American Biography.* Americans no longer living.

(4) *Who's Who in Britain.* Prominent living Britons; 1848 to date; annual.

(5) *Current Biography.* Backgrounds of people in the news, published monthly in pamphlet form and later compiled into bound volumes.

(6) *Twentieth Century Authors.* Biographical material on many contemporary authors.

(7) *Living Authors,* H. W. Wilson. Brief biographies.

(8) *Webster's Biographical Dictionary.* Contains more than 40,000 biographical sketches.

(9) *Biography Index.* Where to find biographical information.

C. Literary Handbooks

(1) Bartlett's *Familiar Quotations*. Common quotations traced to their sources in literature. Complete index of author, subject and key word.

(2) Granger's *Index to Poetry and Recitations*. Books and selections arranged in three indexes: title, author and first line. Title index indicates in what book or anthology the selection may be found.

(3) Stevenson's *Home Book of Quotations*. Quotations listed from poetry and prose under subject headings.

(4) Stevenson's *Home Book of Verse*. A very inclusive poetry anthology, with an index of title, author and first line.

(5) Crowell's *Handbook for Readers and Writers*. Facts, figures and rules to help writers; famous characters and technical terms to help readers.

(6) Brewer's *Dictionary of Phrase and Fable*. Common phrases and allusions traced to their source. Includes colloquial and proverbial phrases, mythological and biblical references, fictitious characters, titles.

(7) Roget's *Thesaurus of English Words and Phrases*. Words and their synonyms listed, with many different shades of meaning, according to the ideas they express. Antonyms are given in an opposite column on the same page. Index at the end gives every word, with its page number, in alphabetical order.

(8) Merriam-Webster's *Dictionary of Synonyms*. Explains the differences in meaning of the synonyms under each entry, and lists their antonyms.

(9) Fowler's *Dictionary of Modern English Usage*. Up-to-date rules for the accepted usage of words.

(10) Benet's *The Reader's Encyclopedia*. Plots, brief biographies of writers, etc.

(11) Trease's *Concise Etymological Dictionary* gives complete history of most English words and shows how their meanings have changed.

D. Atlases

Atlases, in addition to their maps, present valuable information about topography, climate, important places, economic and historical developments. Check the copyright date before using an atlas, because the international picture is fluid. Here are some of the atlases available for reference:

(1) Webster's *Geographical Dictionary*.

(2) Collier's *World Atlas & Geography*.

(3) *The Encyclopaedia Britannica Atlas*.

(4) Goode's *World Atlas*.

(5) Hammond's *Universal World Atlas*.

(6) Rand McNally *Cosmopolitan World Atlas*.

E. Current Information

(1) *World Almanac and Book of Facts*. An annual handbook that summarizes the world events of the past year and contains facts and statistics on every subject—from the batting average of Babe Ruth to the number of eggs produced in Oklahoma.

(2) *Information Please Almanac*. An inclusive reference book of world facts and a review of events of the year.

(3) *Statesman's Year-Book*. Information about countries and governing bodies.

(4) *The Readers' Guide to Periodical Literature*. An up-to-date index to articles from over a hundred magazines. Published semi-monthly from September to June, and monthly in July and August, it is later bound in annual and triennial volumes. It tells you where articles can be found by listing subjects, authors and titles.

F. Using the *Readers' Guide*

The *Readers' Guide to Periodical Literature* (New York, H. W. Wilson Co.) is probably the most valuable source of current information on any topic. The *Readers' Guide* is issued every three months. Each issue covers material published in periodicals during the previous three months. Every three years, these issues are gathered into a bound volume. In going through the *Readers' Guide*, it is useful to remember that all the articles listed there are listed under both the author's name and under the name of the subject covered by the article.

ARCHITECTURE, Modern
He adds elegance to modern architecture:
P. Johnson. A. L. Huxtable. il N Y Times
Mag p 18-19+ My 24 '64 ————————— **Date of issue.**
Philip Johnson. C. Amory. il Vogue 143:184-
92+ My '64
ARCHIVES
United States
Archival product of a century of federal as-
sistance to agriculture. H. T. Pinkett. bib-
liog f Am Hist R 69:689-706 Ap '64 ———— **Name of periodical.**
ARENDT, Hannah
Hannah Arendt on Eichmann. N. Podhoretz.
Commentary 36 201-8 S '63; Discussion. 37: —— **Page numbers.**
6+ F: 16+ My '64
ARGENTINA
Argentina: a study in self-contempt. L. ———— **Article's title.**
Gross. il Look 28:74-7 Je 2 '64
See also
Fishing—Argentina
Labor and laboring classes—Argentina
Economic conditions
Argentina's problems. H. Hazlitt. Newsweek —— **Article's author.**
63:84 My 11 '64
See also
Argentina—Industries
Industries
Argentina: inflation in the midst of a reces-
sion. il Bsns W p54 My 2 '64 ——————— **Article is illustrated.**
ARGONNE, Battle of the, 1918. See European
war, 1914-1918—Campaigns and battles
ARKANSAS
Politics and government
Coming up: a two-party fight in Arkansas. ——— **Volume number of**
il U S News 56:20 My 4 '64 **periodical.**
ARMAMENTS
Free world split will widen. E. Stillman. il
Nations Bsns 52:34-5+ Ap '64 ——————— **Article continued in**
back of issue.

Selections from the *Readers' Guide to Periodical Literature*

6. LOOKING UP SPECIFIC BOOKS

After checking your library's general reference books, your next step should be to find out whether the library has any specific books that would give you helpful material. How can you find out if there are available books that you could look into?

Every book that the library owns is listed on an index card. These index cards are assembled in the *card catalogue*. The card catalogue can tell you immediately whether the library owns a copy of the book you want. (The librarian, and not the card catalogue, will tell you whether the book is in the library or has been borrowed.)

How can the card catalogue tell you where to look for the book on the shelves?

A. The Dewey Decimal System

The Dewey Decimal System, created in 1876 by Melvil Dewey, a New York librarian, classifies library books (except fiction and biography) into 10 classes with numbers which identify them on the shelves.

According to this plan books are grouped into ten classes:

000-099	General works (reference books, encyclopedias, bound periodicals, almanacs)
100-199	Philosophy, psychology, conduct
200-299	Religion, mythology
300-399	Social sciences, economics, government, law, education
400-499	Language (includes dictionaries, grammars)
500-599	Natural sciences (mathematics, astronomy, biology, etc.)
600-699	Useful arts (includes agriculture, engineering, sewing, gardening)
700-799	Fine arts (includes sculpture, painting, music)
800-899	Literature (includes poetry, plays, essays)
900-999	History (includes geography, travel)

Each of these classes has subdivisions. For example, literature is divided into:

800-809	General
810-819	American literature
820-829	English literature

830-839	German literature
840-849	French literature
850-859	Italian literature
860-869	Spanish literature
870-879	Latin literature
880-889	Greek literature
890-899	Literature of other languages

There are additional subdivisions, so that under American literature or English literature, we have special numbers designating poetry, drama, fiction, essays, oratory, letters, satire and humor. By the use of decimals, the numbers are broken down further. Early English Drama 1066-1400, for instance, is 822.1.

These numbers are called the *class numbers.* They are combined with the initial of the author's last name to give the *call number.* The call number is the number by which a book is classified.

Some libraries use a system of their own or the Library of Congress system. However, whichever system is used, the most important key to the location of any book in a library is the "call number."

Small libraries keep their card catalogues as simple as possible. Some libraries have an *Author Card,* a *Title Card* and a *Subject Card* for each book they own. In some cases the title of the book is to be found also on the author's card for simplification and easy reference. In the upper left-hand corner of these cards is the *call number* which directs you to the shelves where books of this number class are stored.

B. Author Card

If you know the author's name you can locate the title of any of his books that are in the library. The titles of books written by one author are arranged in alphabetical order under the author's name.

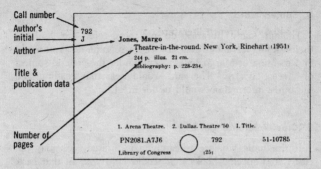

C. Title Card

If you do not know the author's name, but you do know the title of the book, you can find both title and author on the title card. Title cards are placed in alphabetical order according to the first word of the title of the book, except for the articles *A*, *An* or *The*.

Last Days of Pompeii, The

Old Wives' Tale, An

The information about Margo Jones's book, shown above on the author's card, would appear thus on the title card:

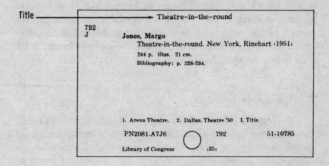

D. Subject Card

Though many libraries do not cross-refer the cards in their catalogues under general headings, some do. You might find mention of Margo Jones's book under the general subject of "Arena Theatre." The card would bear that heading, and the other information would be identical.

E. Cross-Reference Card

If the topic you are researching is limited, you may not easily find specific books that would help you. In that case, look in related fields. Cards which say "see" or "see also" will guide you in directions that may prove fruitful.

Such tips are given you on the author's card, in the case of Margo Jones's book. Although the "see also" is missing, the suggestion is very clear that you should investigate further books on "Arena Theatre," and "Dallas, Theatre '50." These clues are often very rewarding.

F. The Magazine File

After researching the card catalogue, look next into the *Readers' Guide to Periodical Literature* which lists magazine articles. Are there any articles that might shed light on your topic? Check with the librarian to learn whether the magazines containing those articles are available. Make a careful record of the titles and dates of unavailable magazines because you might find them in another library or at home, or be able to borrow them from friends.

G. Newspaper Index

The New York Times Index offers a complete index to articles that have appeared in *The New York Times* referring to people and events. Some libraries own bound copies of the newspapers in which you can look for current information.

H. Local Experts

Are there people in your own town who are experts on the subject you have chosen to write about? A football or baseball coach, for instance, could give you excellent information for a report on sports. Your police chief could help you if you're researching traffic problems. The manager of your local factory could steer you in the right direction if your topic is automation or assembly-line production.

An interview with such people would not only be helpful, but might arouse your curiosity and your enthusiasm about your subject even more, and encourage you to get on with it. Knowing as much as you already do about your topic in a general way, you can jot down a list of questions you'd like to ask in a personal interview. Write a letter to the person or persons you choose, or make a phone call requesting an interview. Set a date, keep it on time, and be ready to ask specific questions.

I. Business Firms

You might also want to write to manufacturers or industrial firms as soon as you've made a rough outline of your topic. If you're writing about designing cars, what better source is there than the engineering department of an automobile manufacturer? Write clear and polite letters requesting information. A general request may draw only booklets. Specific questions will get specific answers.

Don't put off such letters until the last minute, however. You may not get an immediate reply. And should it come late, you may be puzzled over how to use the interesting material without upsetting your whole outline.

J. The U.S. Government Printing Office

The U. S. Government publishes pamphlets on thousands of different subjects. Write to the Superintendent of Documents, Government Printing Office, Washington 25, D. C., stating the exact topic you are researching, and asking for a list of publications on this subject. From that list you can order the pamphlets you think would be of most help to you.

7. READING SOURCE MATERIAL AND TAKING NOTES

A. Reading Source Material

Up to now we've said nothing about recording the location of source material you think would be helpful, or taking notes for your report. You will need several packs of 3 x 5 ruled file cards, for you will make all your notes on cards. They are easy to handle and stand up better than pieces of paper. A bound notebook makes an impossible job out of sorting and arranging notes. Have plenty of cards because you will write only on one side of each card. This makes sorting easier and prevents the omission of information that can get lost on the back of a card.

For every source book you use, you will make out a bibliography card, like this:

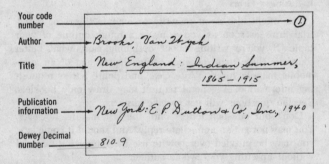

Your code
number

Author ——— Brooks, Van Wyck

Title ——— New England : Indian Summer,
1865 – 1915

Publication
information ——— New York: E. P. Dutton & Co., Inc., 1940

Dewey Decimal
number ——— 810.9

Notice the circled number in the upper right-hand corner of the card. This is your personal code number for referring to this book when you take notes from it. By using this number on your note card you can speedily identify the source of your notes without bothering to write out the full title and author's name every time you take notes on the book.

Copy the details clearly and accurately on your bibliography cards because you will need them later when you are preparing the final draft of your report. It's a great nuisance to have to look this sort of thing up a second time. So get it clearly and accurately down on your card the very first time.

If you do, however, want to look again for the book, the number in the lower left-hand corner will help you find it quickly on the library shelves. This is the Dewey Decimal number which identifies the spot where the book can be found.

Make a bibliography card for each encyclopedia, dictionary, reference book, magazine or book reference you use. Here are sample bibliography cards for the various types of research sources you might use for your report:

(1) An encyclopedia article:

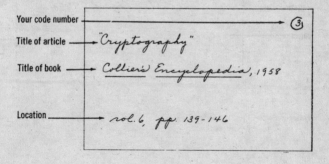

Your code number ———————————————— ③

Title of article ——→ "Cryptography"

Title of book ——→ Collier's Encyclopedia, 1958

Location ——→ vol. 6, pp. 139-146

18

(2) A dictionary:

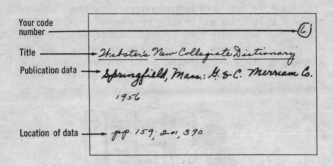

Your code number ────────────────────────► 6.

Title ────► *Webster's New Collegiate Dictionary*

Publication data ──► Springfield, Mass.: G. & C. Merriam Co.

1956

Location of data ──► pp. 159, 201, 390

(3) A signed magazine article:

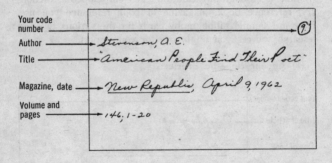

Your code number ────────────────────────► 9.

Author ────► Stevenson, A. E.

Title ────► "American People Find Their Poet"

Magazine, date ──► *New Republic*, April 9, 1962

Volume and pages ──► 146, 1–20

(4) A signed newspaper article:

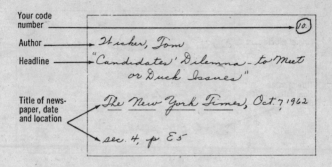

Your code number —————————————————→ (10.)

Author ————→ Tucker, Tom

Headline ————→ "Candidates' Dilemma - to Meet or Duck Issues"

Title of newspaper, date and location ————→ The New York Times, Oct. 7, 1962

————→ sec. 4, p. E5

(5) An unsigned newspaper article:

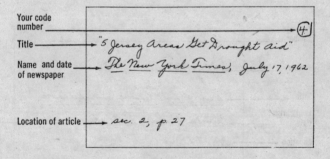

Your code number —————————————————→ (41)

Title ————→ "5 Jersey Areas Get Drought Aid"

Name and date of newspaper ————→ The New York Times, July 17, 1962

Location of article ————→ sec. 2, p. 27

20

(6) An unsigned magazine article:

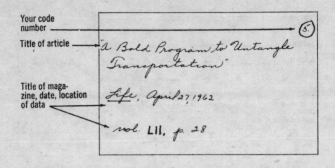

Your code number ────────────→ (5.)

Title of article ────── "A Bold Program to Untangle Transportation"

Title of magazine, date, location of data ────→ *Life*, April 27, 1962

────→ vol. LII, p. 28

(7) A book by one author:

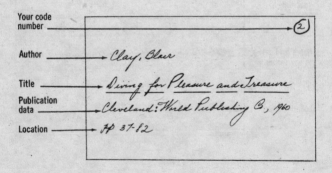

Your code number ────────────→ (2.)

Author ────→ Clay, Blair

Title ────→ Diving for Pleasure and Treasure

Publication data ────→ Cleveland: World Publishing Co., 1960

Location ────→ pp. 37-82

(8) A book by more than one author:

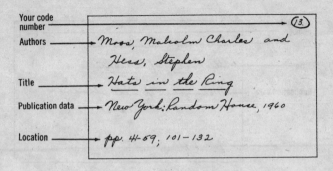

Your code number → ⑬

Authors → Moss, Malcolm Charles and Hess, Stephen

Title → Hats in the Ring

Publication data → New York: Random House, 1960

Location → pp. 4-59; 101-132

(9) A book that is edited:

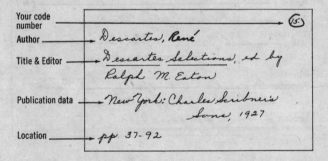

Your code number → ⑮

Author → Descartes, René

Title & Editor → Descartes Selections, ed. by Ralph M. Eaton

Publication data → New York: Charles Scribner's Sons, 1927

Location → pp. 37-92

(10) An anthology:

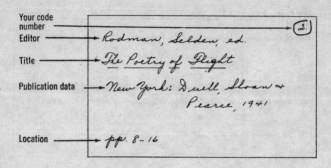

Your code number → ②

Editor → Rodman, Selden, ed.

Title → The Poetry of Flight

Publication data → New York: Duell, Sloan & Pearce, 1941

Location → pp. 8-16

(11) A pamphlet in a series:

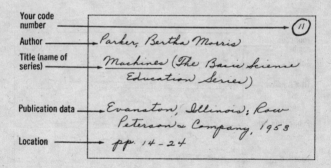

Your code number → ⑪

Author → Parker, Bertha Morris

Title (name of series) → Machines (The Basic Science Education Series)

Publication data → Evanston, Illinois: Row Peterson & Company, 1953

Location → pp. 14-24

(12) An unsigned pamphlet:

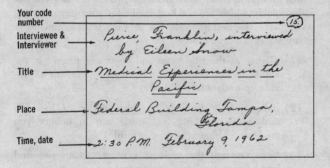

Your code number ⟶ ⑧

Name of organization that published pamphlet ⟶ *General Motors Corporation*

Title ⟶ *Power Goes to Work*

Publication data ⟶ *Detroit, Michigan, 1945*

(13) An interview:

Your code number ⟶ ⑮

Interviewee & Interviewer ⟶ *Pierce, Franklin, interviewed by Eileen Snow*

Title ⟶ *Medical Experiences in the Pacific*

Place ⟶ *Federal Building Tampa, Florida*

Time, date ⟶ *2:30 P.M. February 9, 1962*

When you have put your personal code number in the upper right-hand corner of each bibliography card, arrange your cards numerically. When the entire book has been read for your report, you need not put in page references. But if only certain sections of the book are helpful for your report, be sure to put the pages involved on your bibliography card.

You could also insert at the bottom of the card certain clues for your own benefit. If a book contains good stories, note that fact on your card. If the diagrams, statistics—even points of view—sound on first reading that they might fit into your report, make a note of the details to make it easier to locate them when you start your serious reading.

Having looked the field over and located considerable material that you might use, pick out the most valuable sources and take the books out of the library for closer study.

B. Reading Tips

You may be tempted to linger over every book you investigate for possible useful material. But since you have so much ground to cover, here are some tips for helping you decide quickly which are the best books for your purpose. You must make the best possible use of each source, and cover many books in a brief time.

(1) Glance at the title page and copyright page. (Is the author an authority? Is the book recent enough to provide up-to-date information?)

(2) Skim quickly through the introduction. (Does the author say anything that leads you to believe you might find his point of view helpful?)

(3) Skim through the table of contents. (Can you find listed any material you might use?)

(4) Skim through subheads before reading whole chapters. (Would specific paragraphs be of use when the whole chapter might not?)

(5) Skim through the list of illustrations, if any. (Would they provide interesting material for your report?)

(6) Study the bibliography carefully. (Does the author suggest other books related to your subject?)

(7) Skim through the appendix. (Is helpful material to be found here?)

(8) Skim through the index. (Is material related to your topic included under other headings in this book?)

(9) When using atlases or current information references check the publication date. (Is this information as up-to-date as possible?)

You will notice that we have suggested that you skim quickly in your preliminary search for useful material. When you skim-read, your eyes must run quickly down a page searching for the key word, the number, or the detail that you want. Don't waste time over any other words. Don't even try to understand what you're skimming. Don't let your eyes shift right and left; skim right through the middle of the page as fast as you can. When your eyes light on the detail you're searching for, stop then, and then only, to read closely.

For every research source you are seriously considering, skim through it first quickly. Study the parts that seem useful. Then take accurate, clear notes. Review the reference to be sure that you have really caught the gist of it and have noted it correctly.

C. Taking Notes

Start with a fresh pack of file cards, your pen or pencil, and your rough outline of your report. Record each separate bit of information on a separate file card. Use one side of the card only. Be sure to insert your personal code number in the upper right-hand corner of your card before you start to write. You might otherwise forget to record the source of your note.

Here are two efficient ways of coding cards:

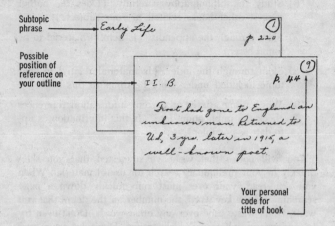

Subtopic phrase

Possible position of reference on your outline

Your personal code for title of book

Early Life

① p. 220

⑨ p. 44

II. B.

Frost had gone to England an unknown man. Returned to U.S. 3 yrs. later in 1915, a well-known poet.

Note the important clues on these cards. The number in the upper right-hand corner identifies your *source*—the book or magazine article from which the material was taken. This number corresponds with the number on one of your bibliography cards—the card that lists all the publishing information about the book or article. The page number is given so you can refer to the exact page should you need to look it up again.

You can take your choice between using a key phrase or a numeral to explain to yourself how and where you plan to use this bit of information in your report. This clue will help you sort out your note cards quickly into separate piles after you have finished reading and start to organize your material.

The only difference between the cards actually is the use of a phrase (called a *slug*) instead of continually referring to your rough outline for a possible position number. The advantage of using slugs is that you can add subtopics without constantly revising and consulting your outline as you work.

However, the code phrases may vary from one card to another, thus complicating your final sorting job. Coding with outline numbers and reworking your outline as you read will give you an outline that needs less revision when you finish your research.

Try both coding methods to see which works better for you. But try them on two separate reports. If you mix the two coding methods on one report, you may be in hopeless confusion when you try to sort your note cards.

D. The Quality of Your Notes

Card-coding, while important for efficiency, is just a mechanical device. The quality of your notes is the important thing.

Make each note brief, but complete and accurate. If you cut too many corners you may omit necessary information. If you make up a sort of shorthand for yourself, you may end with an unintelligible set of hieroglyphics. Here, for instance, is a note card that may have made sense the day it was written down, but is far from understandable when the moment comes later to use the information.

Jot down phrases, lists or rough outlines, rather than complete sentences. This saves space and time. But make what you write now usable later on.

Most important of all: *write your notes in your own words.* If you copy sentences and phrases directly from your sources, your finished report will sound like a patchwork of other people's writing rather than your own. If you do copy a sentence to quote in your report, be sure to copy it exactly and to enclose it in quotation marks. A few quotations can be effective in referring to experts' opinions. Too many quotes will give the impression that you are filling up your report with others' words because you're afraid your own can't stand alone. Never use quotations for factual material. Facts of general knowledge should always be reorganized and written in your own words.

Limit yourself to taking notes only on the facts you will need for your report. Don't waste time or clutter your cards with useless information.

E. Tips on Note Taking

(1) Write down *all* the information you will need, and *get it the first time around*.

(2) Write *clearly* so you can read your own handwriting later on.

(3) *Abbreviate* wherever you can, but make such shortcuts understandable.

(4) Make your notes *full*, so you will have enough source information for your footnotes and bibliography.

(5) Make your notes *exact*, so that you can quote or paraphrase accurately on your final draft.

(6) *Condense* your notes into main ideas rather than a welter of details.

(7) *Organize* your note taking so that you stick closely to your rough outline.

(8) *Arrange* your note cards from time to time so you can see how closely you are sticking to your topic, or how far afield your reading is leading you. This gives you a chance to fill in parts of your outline that seem to be skimpy.

Be sure to write on only one side of a card. If your note runs over to a second card, number them so you will not lose the sequence. Better still, staple them together at one corner.

8. REVISING YOUR ROUGH OUTLINE

By the time you have finished your research reading, you will know quite a bit about your particular subject. You may also have the feeling that dozens of facts and bits of interesting information are floating helter-skelter around in your mind. This is a good time to take a short vacation from your report.

After several days of letting your report "cook on the back of the stove" try to draft the general pattern you think it should take. Do this without referring to your note cards or to your rough outline. Simply jot down the five or six main ideas that stand out as most important in your mind. Rearrange them in logical order. Do not be concerned at this point with subtopics.

Ask yourself if your general pattern of ideas will accomplish the purpose of your report. After all, this research paper of yours is a study of a subject which sets out with a definite purpose to accomplish a certain end.

Do your main ideas fall into chronological order? Should, therefore, your report start with the earliest date and move through the days, months or years to the concluding date? Do your thoughts seem to fall into a step-by-step pattern? Are there pro's and con's to your subject, so that it would be reasonable to give first the arguments for, then those against, before coming to your own conclusion?

Put your thoughts in shape without digging back into your variety of subtopics. Once your general pattern is on paper, sort out your note cards. Put all the cards with the same slug

or outline number together. After sorting your cards, decide
how closely this new general pattern of yours resembles the
rough outline you started with.

Next decide which are main ideas and which are subtopics.
Then measure approximately the size of your various piles of
cards. This will give you a preliminary guess as to whether
your material gathering has been lopsided or fairly evenly
divided.

Write each of your main ideas at the top of a separate sheet
of paper. Arrange these main ideas in logical order, and number them in sequence. Check this arrangement with both your
original rough outline and the new general pattern your
thoughts took. If necessary, change the sequence of main
ideas in this revised outline. With this new skeleton settled
on, fit each of your subtopics into its proper place under the
main idea to which it applies. Write your subtopics on your
numbered papers, after carefully considering the order in
which they should go. Number your subtopics. When you
have finished this arranging and rearranging, your revised
outline will be complete.

Electing a President

I. Political parties.
    A. Major parties.
    B. Minor parties.
    C. Primary elections.

II. Election machinery.
    A. Precinct workers.
    B. Registration.
    C. Absentee ballots.
    D. Voting requirements.

III. Nominating conventions.
    A. Delegates.
        1. Who they are.
        2. How chosen.
    B. Party platform.
    C. Nomination.

IV. The Campaign (and the issues).
    A. Party workers.
    B. Newspapers.
        1. Partisan.
        2. Endorsements.
    C. Radio and TV.
    D. Public opinion polls.

V. Electoral college.
    A. Historical background.
    B. Mechanics

VI. Election day.
    A. At the polls.
        1. Poll watchers.
        2. Challengers.
        3. Machines & hand-marked ballots.
    B. Counting the ballots.
        1. Acknowledging defeat.
        2. Radio and TV.

Here are the important points to remember about outlining:

(1) Numbers and letters alternate.
   a. Main topics are shown by Roman numerals.
   b. Important details under Roman numerals are shown by capital letters.
   c. Details under the capital letters are shown by Arabic numerals.
   d. Details under the Arabic numerals are shown by small letters.
(2) The first word of each point should be capitalized.
(3) Any point that has subpoints must have at least two, since you cannot divide anything into fewer than two parts.
(4) Each number and capital letter should be followed by a period.
(5) Use with complete sentences or topics after each number and letter; but do not mix the two in one outline.

Study the filled-in outline of the body of your paper, then fill in the second and third parts in a similar way:

I. First main topic.
   A. Important detail about I.
   B. Another important detail about I.
      1. Detail about B.
      2. Another detail about B.
         a. Detail about 2.
         b. Another detail about 2.
         c. Still another detail about 2.
II.
   A.
   B.
      1.
      2.
      3.
III.
   A.
      1.
      2.

You can see how subtopics have been put into their places. Main ideas have been shifted around for better order. The skeleton of the basic rough outline has been filled in with appropriate details.

After you've put the "flesh" on the "bones" of your outline, examine your note cards. Do you have enough material on each main idea and each subtopic? Did you skip one and go overboard on another? Does the weight of your material on one subtopic really mean that it is more important than another?

Now is the time to fill in the gaps in your research. Your revised outline and your piles of note cards will make it obvious where you must add to the material you have already gathered. So go back to the library and limit yourself rigidly to looking up just the phase of your subject that you skimped on before.

You may be tempted to toss out a subtopic on which you have little information rather than do more research reading. If the subtopic is important in the logical development of your report, don't eliminate it just because your research was incomplete. Dig deeper and wider for the information you need.

And be careful not to clutter up your report with material that doesn't really belong in it, just because you happen to have notes available. Discard such note cards. Don't throw them away—just put aside cards that do not seem to fit in logically anywhere. They may later find their rightful places as you begin to write, and as you revise your writing. They may even come in handy as footnotes.

9. WRITING YOUR FIRST DRAFT

With your revised outline in front of you, write your first draft at top speed. Write as clearly and simply as you can. Put your thoughts down on paper in direct sentences and well-constructed paragraphs. Concoct transitional sentences to link one paragraph to the next. Write transitional paragraphs to connect one main thought with another.

Don't slow yourself down by worrying over whether you have just the perfect introduction, whether your spelling is completely accurate (underline words you're doubtful about to remind yourself to look them up later). Your sentences may be choppy or they may be long and involved. Don't stop to change them now. You can revise and polish them later. Your main job now is to translate your notes into clearly expressed thoughts that will register with your reader.

As you go along, make notations showing where you will want to insert footnotes. Footnotes are necessary when you use another writer's ideas, whether you quote him directly or indirectly, and when you use diagrams, statistics or other factual data found in source books. You can also use a footnote to insert additional information that is interesting, but is merely a sidelight on the main idea you are discussing.

In writing your first draft longhand, leave wide margins and wide spaces between the lines. Use just one side of the paper, and number the pages in order. You'll be doing your revision on this copy, remember.

But before settling down to correcting it, put it aside to "cool" for several days. You're too close to it at this point to see how it should be polished. So take a vacation from it, then come back to it fresh and unprejudiced. You'll be able to tackle the job of editing it almost as though it were someone else's report and you had never had a thing to do with it. You will need that "cold, fishy" eye to catch little errors and to smooth out your style and construction.

10. REVISING YOUR FIRST DRAFT

When you sit down to work on your report again, read it straight through rapidly to get the feel of it in its entirety. That quick reading will point out some of the big flaws, such as faulty sequence of ideas or clumsy relationships between paragraphs. Put question marks beside such places in the margin as you go along.

There are other marks, called proofreader's marks that you can insert on your first draft as you go along.

A. Proofreader's Marks

Mark	Example	Meaning
¶		Paragraph
no ¶		No paragraph
⩘ ⩘;		Insert comma, insert semicolon
tr	Steamsh~pi~	Transpose
ℓ	Indian ~Summer~	Take out
stet	~quoted~ by	Let it stand
[		Move to left
]		Move to right
ℓc	*T*ransportation	Lower case (small letter)
uc	people	Upper case (capital letter)
	the ∧deep oceans	Insert word
#	∧deep∧sea	Insert space
⌒	sound ⌒ing	Close up
⊙	illus∧	Insert period

B. Your Style of Writing

With the whole paper in your mind, ask yourself whether you have accomplished in this paper what you set out to do. Is the subject you chose for your topic developed logically from introduction to conclusion? Have you presented your ideas clearly and simply?

Be ruthless with your own words. Just because you wrote them, don't be afraid to cut them out. Dare to change them for better words. Slash whole paragraphs if you feel they add nothing, or rewrite them differently. Take the humdrum and ordinary words out of your report and replace them with live-ly, colorful and equally efficient words that you can find in the thesaurus or the dictionary.

Make most of these corrections directly on the pages of your first draft. It will save you considerable copying time. If you rewrite a section here or there, write it on separate paper and staple the paper to the spot in which it is to be inserted.

11. HOW TO USE DIRECT QUOTATIONS

In writing your research paper, you will frequently have to quote what other people have said on your subject. Often, too, when analyzing what others have said in writing, you will have to reproduce portions of their written statements word for word in your own paper so that the reader can follow your reasoning.

When quoting what other people have written, follow these rules: (1) All quotations should be indented one inch from the left-hand margin. (2) If the quote is over sixty words long, single-space it, and do not enclose it in quotation marks. (3) If the quote is under sixty words, double-space it and enclose it in quotation marks. (4) When quoting verse, copy the verse exactly as you find it. Single-space it except for a double space between stanzas, and try to center it on the page. Do not use quotation marks. (5) All quotations should be foot-noted.

If, to preserve space, you want to omit part of the quotation, and doing so will not change the author's original meaning, you may indicate the omission by using ellipsis marks (three spaced periods . . .). If the omission is at the end of a sentence, add the appropriate punctuation after the ellipsis marks. If you wish to insert your own comment into the middle of a quotation, enclose your comment in brackets. If, in the quotation, there is another quotation, the quotes inside the quotes should be enclosed in single quotation marks:

"After the flood . . . he [Jim] said, 'Go back to your homes.' "[1]

12. ORGANIZING FOOTNOTES

The whole point of footnotes is to give credit to the source of a fact or a theory that you have referred to in your report. When you use someone else's ideas or phrasing without giving him credit you are *plagiarizing* (stealing). In your report you will want to be completely honest, so you will acknowledge every source from which you are using material.

Factual information or quotations that are general knowledge need no footnotes. Use a footnote to:

1. Give credit for a direct quotation.
2. For an original or unusually interesting opinion or interpretation.
3. For statistics or figures.

Footnotes are also useful to give a definition, contrary opinion, or explanation that might otherwise interrupt or clutter up your report.

There is no fixed requirement as to how many footnotes each page of a report must have. It depends entirely upon the subject matter. Some pages may carry five or six footnotes at the bottom of the page, and others may have only one or two.

There are various forms for footnotes and, unless your teacher has a definite preference, any of the standard forms are correct. Footnotes must, however, be consistent throughout your report, and be clear and easy to read.

Here is a typical collection of footnotes of various kinds that you might find at the bottom of a page of a research paper:

[1]Henry Louis Mencken, <u>The American Language</u>, 4th ed.; New York: Alfred A. Knopf, Inc., 1936, p. 168.

This footnote shows how to refer to a book. The number, called a *superscript,* is placed above and to the left of the author's full name, beginning with his first name. The title of the book is underlined. (On the typewriter it is underlined; when printed, it is in italics.) If there is a special edition, its number comes next, followed by the place of publication, the publisher's full name, the date of publication, then the page reference.

[2]"Personality Tests," *Life*, XXI, October 7, 1964, p. 55.

This footnote shows how to refer to a magazine article, the author of which is not known. The title of the article is placed between quotation marks, the name of the magazine is underlined (in italics when printed), followed by the volume number in Roman numerals, date of magazine, and page reference. Had the name of the author been known, his name would have been given first, followed by the name of his article.

[3]Ibid.

Ibid., an abbreviation of the Latin word *ibidem,* means "in the same place." When a footnote refers to exactly the same source as the footnote immediately preceding it, *ibid.* is used. It means that the footnote refers to the same page of the same book by the same author.

[4]Ibid., p. 59.

When *ibid.* is followed by a different page number, it means that the reference is still to the same book by the same author, but on another page.

[5]Mencken, p. 240.

This footnote refers to a different page of the same book by Mencken mentioned in the first footnote.

Here are some helpful abbreviations used in writing research papers. They will also help you in understanding these abbreviations when you are doing the research for your paper.

anon.	anonymous; the author is not known.
art.	article.
c. or ca.	*circa;* at, in or approximately; referring to dates.
chap.	chapter; plural, chaps.
e.g.	*exempli gratia;* Latin, "for example."
et seq.	*et sequens, et sequentes;* Latin, meaning "and the one following," "and those that follow."
fig.	figure; plural, figs.
i.e.	*id est;* Latin, meaning, "that is."
n.	note; plural, nn.
op. cit.	*opere citato;* Latin, meaning "in the work cited or quoted."
p.	page; plural, pp.
sec.	section; plural, secs.
v.	volume; plural, vols.

When you have finished rereading and correcting your second version of your paper, it is a good idea to insert all footnotes directly on your revised copy. You might otherwise forget to include them when you are making your final copy. You might also forget to leave enough space for them at the bottom of the page. If you present all your footnotes in a block at the end of your paper, you should entitle them "notes"—*not* "footnotes."

Place an Arabic numeral above and to the right of the work or the sentence requiring the footnote, thus[1]. The next footnote will be numbered[2], and so on throughout the report. As you have seen, each footnote number is repeated at the bottom of the page below a short line that separates footnotes from text.

The first time a reference source is credited in a footnote, it must be clearly identified, and it should follow this form:

A book by one author:

[1]Henry Louis Mencken, The American Language, 4th ed. ; New York: Alfred A. Knopf, Inc. , 1936, p. 168.

An anthology:

[2]Tennyson, Alfred, "Lady of Shalott," in
The Home Book of Verse, ed. by B. E. Stevenson,
New York: Henry Holt, 1918, p. 3188.

A book by two or more authors:

[3]Malcolm Charles Moos and Stephen Hess,
Hats in the Ring, New York; 1960, p. 103.

A book that is edited:

[4]René Descartes, Descartes Selections, ed.
by Ralph M. Eaton, New York: 1927, p. 69.

A book in a series:

[5]Richard B. Morris and the Editors of Life,
The Making of a Nation, 1775-1789 (The Life
History of the U.S. Series), New York: Time,
Inc., 1963, vol. 2, p. 146.

A book with no author's name given:

[6]Who's Who, 1965, London: A. & C. Black,
Ltd., 1965, p. 991.

An encyclopedia article:

[7]"Cryptography," Collier's Encyclopedia,
1958, vol. 6, p. 139.

A signed magazine article:

[8]Siler Freeman, "Driver Education: It Saves
Lives," Look, XXVI, May 22, 1962, p. 116.

An unsigned magazine article:

[9]"A Bold Program to Untangle Transportation," <u>Life</u>, LII, April 27, 1962, p. 28.

A signed news article:

[10]Henry Tanner, "Soviet Cautions on Arming Bonn in Atomic Fleet," <u>The</u> <u>New</u> <u>York</u> <u>Times</u> July 13, 1964 , sec. 1, p. 1.

An unsigned news article:

[11]"Dominican Crisis and the U.S. Role," <u>The</u> <u>New</u> <u>York</u> <u>Times</u>, May 2, 1965, sec. 4, p. 1.

A signed pamphlet:

[12]David D. Burks, <u>Cuba</u> <u>Under</u> <u>Castro</u>, Foreign Policy Association, "Headline Series," no. 165, New York, June 20, 1964, p. 1.

An unsigned pamphlet:

[13]The Commerce and Industry Institute, Inc., <u>A</u> <u>Practical</u> <u>Guide</u> <u>to</u> <u>Unemployment</u> <u>Insurance</u> <u>for</u> <u>New</u> <u>York</u> <u>Employers</u>, New York, 1963.

A public document:

[14]U.S. Department of Health, Education, and Welfare, <u>Elementary</u> <u>School</u> <u>Mathematics:</u> <u>New</u> <u>Directions</u>, 1963.

An interview:

[15]John Paul Evans, interviewed by Philip Matson, Hotel Statler, New York City, 11 a.m., June 18, 1965.

A play:

[16]Emmet Lavery, The Magnificent Yankee, Act III, scene 2.

A letter:

[17]Robert Frost, Letter to John Jones, December 8, 1950.

13. YOUR BIBLIOGRAPHY

When you first started doing your research for this paper, you made bibliography cards for each of your sources. Sort these cards now, and arrange them alphabetically by the first letter of the last name of each author. If the author's name is not known (as, for instance, in a magazine editorial) list items alphabetically by the first word (except The, A, An) of the article's title. If you consulted several books by the same author, arrange them chronologically according to their dates of publication. You need not repeat the author's name each time, but can use a half-inch dash instead.

Your bibliography is a list of *all* the sources that you consulted while doing your research. This list can be a simple alphabetical arrangement of authors' names (beginning with the first initial of their surnames), or you can classify the items into books, magazines, newspapers, encyclopedia articles,

etc. Your bibliography comes at the very end of your report,
and is written on a separate page. Here is an example:

"Bold Program to Untangle Transportation," Life,
    LII, April 27, 1962.

Burks, David D., Cuba Under Castro, Foreign
    Policy Assn., "Headline Series," no. 165,
    New York, June 20, 1964.

Commerce and Industry Institute, Inc., A Prac-
    tical Guide to Unemployment Insurance
    for New York Employers, New York, 1963.

"Cryptography," Collier's Encyclopedia, 1958,
    vol. 6.

Descartes, René, Descartes Selections, ed. by
    Ralph M. Eaton, New York: Charles Scrib-
    ner's Sons, 1927.

"Dominican Crisis and the U.S. Role," The New
    York Times, May 2, 1965.

Evans, John Paul, interviewed by Philip Maston,
    Hotel Statler, New York City, 11 a.m.,
    June 18, 1965.

Freeman, Siler, "Driver Education: It Saves
    Lives," Look, XXVI, May 22, 1962.

Frost, Robert, Letter to John Jones, December
    8, 1965.

Lavery, Emmet, The Magnificent Yankee, Act
    III, scene 2.

Mencken, Henry Louis, <u>The American Language,</u>
     4th ed., New York: Alfred A. Knopf, Inc.,
     1936.

Moos, Malcolm Charles and Hess, Stephen, <u>Hats</u>
     <u>in the Ring</u>, New York: Random House, 1960.

Morris, Richard B. and the Editors of <u>Life</u>, <u>The</u>
     <u>Making of a Nation</u>, vol. 2: 1775-1789 (The
     <u>Life</u> History of the U.S. Series), New York:
     Time, Inc., 1963.

Tanner, Henry, "Soviet Cautions on Arming Bonn
     in Atomic Fleet, " <u>The New York Times</u>,
     July 13, 1964.

Tennyson, Alfred, "Lady of Shalott, " in <u>The</u>
     <u>Home Book of Verse,</u> ed. by B.E. Steven-
     son, New York: Henry Holt, 1918.

U.S. Department of Health, Education, and Wel-
     fare, <u>Elementary School Mathematics: New</u>
     <u>Directions</u>, 1963.

<u>Who's Who, 1965,</u> London: A. & C. Black, Ltd., 1965.

14. OTHER MECHANICAL DETAILS

Unless your teacher gives you specific instructions, here are some suggestions for the presentation of your final draft.

Make a *Title Page* which will feature the subject of your report. Make your title as intriguing as possible. Try to arouse your reader's interest before he even starts to read what you've written. A catchy title will do it. Center the title on the page. Below it put your name, class, teacher's name, and the date. This information could also go in the lower left-hand corner of your title page.

For page 2 you might add an *Introduction* or *Preface*, if you have some special comments to make about your research or the presentation of your material. If you interviewed experts, for instance, while you were gathering your material, you could name them and their contribution to your report. If your report is based on a subject about which you knew quite a bit in the beginning—a hobby or science project, for instance— you could explain how you first became interested, and how your research has added to your knowledge of the subject. This introduction should be brief, and written on a separate page.

The final, revised outline that you followed when writing your report should be page 3. This outline serves as a *Table of Contents.*

If you wish to include charts, diagrams, maps or other technical illustrations in your report, add an *Appendix.* Be sure to give credit to the sources from which you took such material.

15. PREPARING YOUR FINAL COPY

Now that all the preparatory work is finished, all that remains to do is make a clean, clear copy of everything you've written. If you must submit a hand-written report, take plenty of time over it, so that every page is neat, the margins are even, the lines are straight, and there are no untidy blots and erasures. A scrawled, careless-looking paper will spoil the whole effect of all your weeks of work.

If you can possibly type your report, do so. It will be more readable and attractive to look at. Your teacher will find it more businesslike.

A. Typing Tips

(1) Double space the text of your report.
(2) Leave a one-line space between footnotes. Single space a two-line footnote. Indent the first line and run the second line flush with the left-hand margin.

(3) Leave one space after a comma or a semicolon.

(4) Leave two spaces after any punctuation mark that ends a sentence; *e.g.*, period, exclamation mark, question mark.

(5) Leave two spaces after a colon when the next word or sentence begins with a capital letter.

(6) Paragraphs are usually indented five spaces. Leave an extra space between paragraphs.

(7) Center the main heading, and for emphasis use all capital letters.

(8) Minor headings can either be centered, or run flush with the left-hand margin. The first letter of each word is capitalized, and the heading is underlined.

(9) Column headings are centered over the longest line in the column. Should, however, this heading be longer than the longest line in the column, the column is centered under the heading.

(10) Figures are usually aligned so that the right margin will be in block form. Written material is usually blocked at the left margin.

(11) Number the pages in the upper right-hand corner.

Here's another valuable tip if you do type your report. Measure very carefully the distance between the footnote numerals in the text and the bottom of the page. It pays to type all footnotes on a separate sheet before you start to type the body of your paper, so you will know exactly how much space they take up. You can allow for this space by marking off the line that will divide the text from the footnotes. By planning ahead of time you can avoid squeezing at the end of a typed page. You can also make very sure that every numeral in the text has its corresponding footnote at the bottom of the page. It's a nuisance to have to type whole pages over just because you forgot to put everything that belongs on that page where it belongs.

When you have copied every part of your report, arrange the sections in this order: title page, introduction, outline, report, appendix, bibliography. Place all the pages together and give them one final reading. Give yourself time to proofread carefully. You need this final check for catching typographical errors, slips in punctuation or minor mistakes in spelling. If you were interrupted constantly while making your final copy, you might even have omitted something important. This final review will show up any errors.

After correcting them, put your pages together inside a folder or stiff paper cover. Label the cover with the title of your report and the name of its author—YOURS.

16. HOW TO WRITE A PRECIS

In school or out of it, you may be asked to write a brief, accurate summary of something you have read. It might be a speech, a short story, a report, a poem, or a whole novel. Anything that isn't already written "tight"—in clear but very concise form—can be summarized in a shorter version.

Writing a précis is an excellent exercise in careful reading and accurate writing. You must, first of all, understand completely what you have read. Then you must state your understanding in the most skillful way you possibly can.

A. What a Précis Is

A précis is a *brief summary of a longer piece of writing expressed in your own words.* It is a condensed version of the essential thought of the original material. It is usually only one-third, perhaps only one-fourth, as long as the original.

B. What a Précis Is Not

A précis is *not a paraphrase of the original writing.* It is not just saying in different and simpler words exactly what the original said.

When you paraphrase a selection, you may write a version that is equally as long as the original. The précis is not as long as a paraphrase.

A précis contains no comment or opinions of your own. It contains no details, no examples, no illustrations. Its language is shorn of unnecessary words.

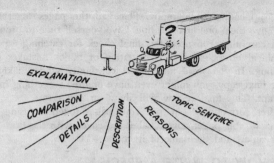

C. The Steps in Writing a Précis

(1) Read the selection carefully. Read it again and again until you are quite sure you understand completely what the author is saying. Search for the writer's main idea. Go through sentence after sentence until you have located the topic sentence. Analyze it closely. Should there be any words or phrases that you do not quite understand, look them up in the dictionary.

(2) As you read, take brief notes on points that seem important to the author. When you have finished reading, read your notes. Do any of them now seem unimportant in view of the main idea? Those will be the points to omit in your précis.

(3) Now write that main idea in your own words. Make it as concise as you can. Do not include ideas or opinions of your own.

(4) Revise your writing to be sure that your version is completely accurate.

(5) Check your version to be sure that the sequence of facts or thoughts is exactly the same as the sequence in the original.

(6) Reread your précis with a view to cutting its length in half.

D. Tips on Shortening Your Précis

You could write a précis that is just one sentence long. But you might not be doing justice to the material you are summarizing. You can, however, cut the extra words from your writing with a view to making your final draft concise yet still clear.

(1) Change clauses to short phrases.

Example: *When he finally reached* the restaurant he found *that his friend had already arrived.*

Cut to: At the restaurant he found *his friend waiting.*

Example: *Since he could not* meet her at the train, he sent his friend *to replace him.*

Cut to: *Unable to* meet her at the train, he sent his friend *instead.*

Example: *If you take* the steak from the freezer now, it will *be thawed out in time for dinner.*

Cut to: *By taking* the steak from the freezer now, it will *thaw by dinnertime.*

(2) Change clauses and phrases to single words.

Example: After *he has graduated,* he will go into the army.

Cut to: After *graduation,* he will go into the army.

Example: My friend *who is a native of Brazil* is coming north for a visit.

Cut to: My *Brazilian* friend is coming north for a visit.

Example: She entertained her sorority sisters *in a gracious manner.*

Cut to: She entertained her sorority sisters *graciously.*

As you can see, there is more than one way to say the same thing. In précis-writing, the shorter the version, the better. Wordiness has no place in a précis. The very meaning of the French word *précis* is "exact," "terse."

E. A Sample Précis

Here is a reading passage followed by four student précis. Three of them are incorrect, inadequate, unsatisfactory. One of them is satisfactory. Read the passage and each of the précis and decide which of the rules were broken, and why the satisfactory version passes all tests.

The great artists of the past, despite the love lavished on them by the scholars and esthetes, are becoming more and more remote and unfamiliar. They are not replaced by others because we are moving into a world of non-art. One has only to compare the world of the long sea voyage, sunsets, leisure, complete works of so-and-so, with the still mildly esthetic world of the train and then with the completely incurious existence of the air-passenger with his few reassuring leaflets issued by the company, his meals wrapped up in cellophane in a cardboard box, his copy of *Time* in case the sleeping pill doesn't work. This unseeing, unreading traveler is a symbol of the new public. Poetry for this civilization may well cease to exist, for no one except a few professors will possess the necessary ear to follow its subtleties. Reading aloud is almost extinct and the poet who wrestles with his subtle tone-effects secures his victories for himself alone. The hopeless are the irresponsible, the irresponsible are the lazy. We must accustom ourselves to a reading public which is both too slothful and too restless to read until a sense of values is restored to it.

(205 words)

Précis 1

The great artists of the past are not being replaced because these days we don't need them. Nobody has time any more for taking long sea voyages, looking at sunsets or reading everything somebody wrote. We're too busy flying in all directions. Speed is our motto. We're hurrying too fast to take time to read. (55 words)

Précis 2

In our day there are no great artists and writers as there were in olden days when artists had rich patrons to support them. The public isn't interested in looking at paintings or reading books any more. People are too busy flying around in all directions to care about art any more. So painters and poets are going out of business. (61 words)

Précis 3

The great artists of the past are becoming remote and unfamiliar and are not being replaced by others because we are moving into a world of non-art. One has only to compare the mildly esthetic days when people traveled by train and had time to read with modern days of airplane travel. Nowadays there is only time to read a few leaflets and skim through *Time* before you are at your destination. Poetry, for instance, may well cease to exist because only a few professors live quietly enough to have the necessary ear for hearing what a poet writes. The reading public is too lazy and too nervous to care. (111 words)

Précis 4

Great artists of the past are not being replaced by comparable modern artists. Our world of non-art is symbolized by the difference between leisurely travel in the past and the rapid, nervous travel of today. The poet finds no large audience to appreciate the fine points of his work. Reading is not the discriminating art it once was, nor will it be again until a sense of values is restored to an irresponsible, lazy reading public. (77 words)

As you read, could you put your finger on the rules that were broken in these précis?

(1) Though this précis was short enough, it missed the main point and emphasized unimportant details.

(2) This précis is also short enough, but the writer injected his own ideas and comments into his writing.

(3) This précis commits two errors. It is too long—over half as long as the original material. It also lifts sentences from the original. A précis must be written in one's own words.

(4) This version is the right length, gets the main point, and summarizes the author's ideas in different words. It is a successful précis.

17. HOW TO WRITE A BOOK REPORT

A book report is half fact and half fancy. The facts are the author's, the fancy is yours. Unlike writing a précis, you should inject your feelings and your opinions into a book report. It is not enough to describe the details of the book. You must express your reactions and your judgment of the book. Your book report should be written from your own point of view.

In reviewing a book, here is the basic outline for your report:

A. The Skeleton of Your Report

1. Introduction
   A. Who is the author? (This is fact.)
   B. What type of book is it? (Also fact.)

2. Plot
   A. Briefly, what is the story about? (Fact.)
   B. How does the story develop? (This is your opinion.)

3. Characters
   A. Who are they? (Fact.)
   B. How are they portrayed? (Your opinion.)

4. Setting
   A. Where, when? (Facts.)
   B. How is it described? (Your opinion.)

5. Style
   A. General characteristics. (Facts.)
   B. How did it appeal to you? (Your feelings.)

6. Summing-up Impression (Your opinion.)

As you can see, the way you feel about the book is as important as the factual account of its details. So we will discuss first of all the expression of your feelings and ideas so that the reader of your report will understand its appeal to you.

B. How to Judge a Novel

When you have closed a book on its last page you have strong feelings of satisfaction, indifference or let-down. Don't let this moment of strongest reaction escape you. It is the best time to jot down a few random notes summing up your feelings about the book.

You may not have time, or even want to write your review then and there. It might be wiser to let your thoughts simmer for a few days before tackling the job of writing your complete report. But while your relationship with the book you have just finished reading is the closest, put some of your thoughts on paper. It may be difficult to recapture them if you wait too long. You certainly don't want your reactions to fade from your mind.

Whether you liked the book or it left you feeling dissatisfied, it is important to get your sensations on paper when your feelings are sharpest. Those scribbled notes of yours may give you a pleasant surprise when you settle down seriously to your report. You will find that you have a headstart. Your notes may give you a complete introductory paragraph or an excellent summarizing conclusion.

Rereading your notes will sharpen the overall impression of the book that has been "jelling" in your mind. Now is the time to ask yourself some questions as you prepare to evaluate the book. Here are some questions to guide you.

(1) *What is the theme of the book?* What message is the author trying to send you? Is the theme clearly expressed and successfully proved? Or does the author present several conflicting themes without proving any of them?

(2) *Does the plot make sense?* Do the incidents follow each other logically and realistically? Are you convinced that such things could happen to these particular characters?

(3) *Do the characters seem like real people to you?* Do you care what happens to them? Are they all beautiful and good? Or do they show their weaknesses and their bad points? Can you believe that each character would really behave as the author shows him behaving? or does the author move his characters around as though they were puppets on strings? What have you learned about human nature in general as a result of meeting these characters?

(4) *Does the dialogue sound real?* Does it tell you about the people who are speaking? Does it reveal their personalities? Do the conversations help to move the story forward and keep it moving? Or does the talk go on and on getting nowhere?

(5) *Does the setting — the time and place — of the story come to life for you?* Can you picture the scenes in your mind's eye? Are the descriptions clear and vivid? Or are they long-winded and dull enough to make you want to skim them to get on with the story? Does the author give enough colorful detail to make this other place come to life?

(6) *Does the style suit the plot and the theme?* Is it clear and simple? Light and amusing? Serious but straightforward? Heavy and wordy? Full of effective figures of speech or humdrum clichés?

As you answer these questions, take notes. Do not be afraid to be critical, but don't criticize for the sake of sounding smart. Note especially one important incident so the reader of your report can sense the flavor and tone of the book. Note a quality of a character — good or bad — that will make your reader feel your enthusiasm or your antagonism toward that character.

Take notes, too, on the "fact" parts of your basic outline. Identify the book and its author. Then arrange your notes in the correct outline form. Have you included too much? Remember, you are not rewriting the book nor giving a blow-by-blow summary of the plot. Your job is to judge the elements of the book and to evaluate it as a whole. One test of a good book report is your success in choosing *significant* details to comment on.

After double-checking your outline and filling in the necessary material, write your first draft. Begin with the factual introduction and wind up with your personal impression of the book as a whole. Revise and polish your first draft carefully to be sure you've included only what should be there and have left out nothing important.

C. How to Judge a Biography

In writing a report on the study of someone's life, the fact items are important, but so too are your answers to the following questions:

(1) *Is the main character presented as an ideal person who is always good and right?* Or do his bad as well as his good qualities show?

(2) *Do the times and the places come to life for you?* Are there enough details to make the setting seem authentic?

(3) *Do you understand how the leading character fitted into his environment?*

(4) *What influenced the growing up of the main character* — his family, his education, his friends, his experiences?

(5) *Is the main character admirable,* despite his weaknesses?

(6) *Did the main character face up to his trials and conflicts and solve them,* or did he side-step them?

(7) *Are the conversations believable and in character?*

(8) *Does the author's style contribute to your pleasure* in the book, or did you keep reading just to find out what happened?

(9) Would you like to know more about the main character or any others portrayed in the book, or was your curiosity completely satisfied?

D. How to Judge History and Current Events

(1) *Does the author present only one viewpoint?* Does he examine various aspects of the background of events, or does he give one simplified explanation?

(2) *Is the background material clear and logical,* or does it confuse you?

(3) *Does the author give a new perspective* on the events he describes? Did your attitude change as you understood better his point of view? Or were you unconvinced?

(4) *Did the author give all the facts?* You can't tell without checking with other authors' accounts of the same events. Did he distort facts to suit his purpose, or omit important details that would have changed the picture entirely?

(5) *Does the author distinguish clearly between the facts and his interpretation of the facts?* Were you able to recognize the differences between them?

(6) *Were you impressed or displeased with the author's style?*

(7) *Was the author qualified to write* about these events or this period? Was he an expert? What was his education and experience?

E. How to Judge a Science Book

(1) *Did you understand the material easily?* If not, was it because the author didn't write clearly? Or was it because you didn't have enough background to make the material understandable?

(2) *Did the author seem to be writing down to you?* Was the material too simplified? Or did he succeed in explaining complicated material clearly enough for you to grasp it?

(3) *Did the author bring material to life for you* by presenting it in terms of human interest? Did he relate science to your everyday life? Or did he make it seem remote and unreal?

(4) *Are the author's facts accurate*, so far as you know?

(5) *Does he supply helpful diagrams, charts, and illustrations* to clarify material?

(6) *What are the author's qualifications for writing this book?* Is he an acknowledged expert in the field, or did he have the help of experts?

F. Writing Your Report

Having read your book and recorded notes on your impressions while they were fresh in your mind, you are ready to assemble your notes for the preparation of your report. You will have the factual material on hand, and your answers to the various questions you asked yourself. These answers may be lengthy. They may emphasize one phase and not another.

Arrange your notes in basic outline form. Include all necessary information; omit details that add little to the picture. Sum up your general impression in the conclusion.

Now write your first draft. Check it thoroughly for correct grammar, usage, spelling and punctuation. Polish your first draft by writing in your corrections. Read it over and over. Does your enthusiasm or dislike for the book carry through to you as it should to the reader of your report? If your report plods along, try to introduce some color and emotion so that your reader will be tempted to investigate the book you read.

G. How to Write a One-Paragraph Review

You may be asked to write only a few full-length reports at school. But you may be required to submit many one-paragraph reviews.

Just off-hand, a one-paragraph review sounds like something you can toss off without much thought. In two or three sentences you can identify the book and say whether you liked it or not, and let it go at that. But it isn't enough.

Being able to write a closely packed summary paragraph will help you in many writing chores — science reports, examinations, business letters, committee reports.

When you have a concise review to write, keep in mind the answers to all of the check-list questions, but plan to use only *some* of the answers. The trick is to select the most important questions — the ones most appropriate for this particular book. By a process of elimination, omit all but the most important comments from your review.

The success of a one-paragraph review depends on the compactness of your thoughts and your sentences. Every idea and every word must count. There is no room for details, descriptions, and dialogue. Your comments must be brief, positive, concrete, and put together in simple, direct sentences.

Arrange your notes in outline form. Study them coldly. Which details are vital to your report and which ones are less important? Can two important details be included in the same sentence? Try it. Can you express your feelings about the main theme in the same sentence? Try it.

Write your first draft as compactly as you can. Go over it word by word to see if you can't condense it even further. Aim at leaving only the gist of the matter intact. Ruthlessly cut out the rest.

Make a clear, clean copy of what is left. Does it make one paragraph? Have you left out something really vital? If you put it back in, will it upset the whole paragraph? Try it.

When you are satisfied that you have written the tightest yet the clearest paragraph possible, make a final copy of it and hand it in.

18. HOW TO WRITE A SCIENCE PROJECT REPORT

Knowing how to write clearly and with authority is just as important for the scientist as it is for the journalist or the scholar. There are two reasons why you should learn how to write good reports of your science projects. First, by putting your work into words, you will gain a better understanding of your project. Second, knowing you are going to write a report of your project and what should be included in the report will help you plan and conduct the project. You will have to apply the same scientific method—the planned, orderly procedures —in writing, as you do in your science work.

The form and content of a science report will vary with the kind of project you are reporting on. Not all of the following items must be included in every report. For example, if a project did not involve an experiment, the written report would not include the items about the reporting of experiments.

A. The Title

A good title will distinguish your project report from all others which have to do with the same general area of study. Titles of scientific reports should convey important information rather than show off the author's cleverness. Thus, the title, "Snakes Are Our Friends," would not be a suitable title for a research project on snakes. It doesn't tell enough, specifically, about the contents of the report. A better title would be, "The Diet of the North American Garter Snake." This title tells exactly what the report is about.

B. Abstract of the Report

A 100- to 150-word summary of the report should follow the title. This summary should include in one paragraph a statement of the purpose of the project, general methods or procedures used, and principal findings and conclusions. The purpose of an abstract is to give the reader enough information for him to decide whether or not to read the whole report.

C. Background Information

This section of the report should give the reader enough information to be able to understand the history and the importance of your problem. It will often include a review of other people's findings. If well written, this section will explain your motives for undertaking the project and will stimulate the reader. Background information may contain references to books and articles, indicated by footnotes. This section is often called simply "Introduction."

D. The Problem

If your report is based on the study of a specific problem, the problem should be clearly stated or defined. You should tell whether you are searching for or testing hypotheses, suggesting a theory, or merely reporting some observations to be made under clearly specified conditions. While discussing the problem, you may often want to show its relationship to other problems. The best reports will include a discussion of the relationship of the problem to existing theories.

E. Hypotheses to Be Tested

If one or a series of experiments is being reported, all hypotheses being tested should be stated. This section may also include a discussion of what the possible experimental results will mean in terms of accepting or rejecting the hypotheses.

F. Procedures

Anyone who reads your report should, with the proper materials and facilities, be able to repeat your experiment or observations and obtain similar results. Therefore, you must describe in detail all of the equipment and conditions (temperature, pressure, or any other environmental factors which could affect the outcome). Photographs and drawings can be used as well as words. Every step in your procedure should be carefully explained. If you discover that some method of doing something will not work, mention it so that others will not repeat your mistake.

G. Data or Observations

Numerical data such as measurements and other statistics are best presented in the form of tables. Observations such as descriptions of flowers or the behavior of animals, should be reported in a simple, logical manner. Frequently such observations are recorded chronologically—in the form of a diary.

H. Analysis and Interpretation of Data or Observations

In simple, short reports, this section may sometimes be included with the preceding one. The analysis of numerical data may include graphs and scattergrams. Statistical methods may be used to discover relationships. Non-mathematical observations should be analyzed and interpreted in terms of the hypotheses that were being tested.

I. Conclusions

In this section, each hypothesis should be reexamined and rejected if the data show it to be wrong. Hypotheses which are supported by the research can be tentatively accepted for further testing. You will seldom be able to fully accept a hypothesis. This section should also, when appropriate, discuss the effect of rejecting or accepting the hypotheses on the theories previously discussed.

J. Implications or Recommendations

This section is sometimes devoted to "generalizations." In this next-to-last section of your report, you should discuss any meaning your research may have for a better understanding of a broad area of science. You should also include a discussion of any new problems (or revisions of hypotheses) that have been suggested by your study. Never try to draw illogical connections between your research results and unrelated areas of interest and study. For example, it would be silly to say, "some foolish people kill our valuable snakes," in a report about "The Diet of the North American Garter Snake."

K. Summary

Always conclude a scientific report with a brief summary of the principal results of your investigation. It is often convenient and desirable to do this by means of a simple opening statement such as "The principal findings of this study were:" and then list the findings.

L. Hints on Style

When writing a scientific report, avoid the use of words which add no scientific understanding to what you are saying. Uncommon words and names should be defined. Use the third person (that is, do not use the words "you" and "I") as much as possible. When in doubt about a word, use a dictionary.

PART II
AN EXAMPLE OF A RESEARCH PAPER

1. A CRITICAL ANALYSIS OF A STUDY OF THE SUN TREADER BY WILLIAM SMITH

This research paper was balanced nicely, in that proper space was devoted to the man Shelley and to the poet as perceived in his verse. The sources, four books and two encyclopedias, were excellent; but perhaps *The Cambridge History of English Literature* and *Moulton's Library of Literary Criticism* should have been consulted. The writing craftmanship was satisfactory except that the number of careless mistakes showed a need for careful proofreading.

The main weakness of the paper was improper technique in research paper form. In one instance there was a glaring example of plagiarism; carelessness is not an excuse. Small errors in footnoting could easily have been avoided. The use of an *ibidem* when there was an intervening footnote showed a faulty grasp of footnoting technique. Also, proper bibliography form was not observed, and the pagination was incorrect in several instances.

A STUDY OF THE SUN TREADER

A Research Paper

Presented to

Mr. Houser of the Department of English

Geneva High School

In Partial Fulfillment

of the Requirements for English Literature

by

William Smith

May 1961

TABLE OF CONTENTS

CHAPTER I

INTRODUCTION

Why Percy Bysshe Shelley? It happened because of the interest aroused in this author through the short biography of him given in the school text. He appealed to the author as a highly sensitive artist, a man who said what he thought or rather wrote it and suffered the consequences. He was different. Different in his life at school where he wouldn't endure traditional hazing, different in life where he loved and married many women and wrote beautiful lines about others, different physically. He is said to have been so beautiful that when Trelawney first saw him he almost mistook Shelley for a girl.[1]

To learn more of Shelley or how he may have come to be the way he was, it was necessary to read of the history of the Shelleys and find out what certain

_____

[1] Shelley, The Encyclopedia Americana 1961 ed., vol. 24, p. 689.

traits were or could have been passed on to him as
explained in ~~my first~~ *the second* chapter. Then his type of education was studied to see what effects this had on
him and his writing. Chapter three deals with his
education. Chapter four tells of Shelley's works. It
does not describe the works themselves but rather
gives ~~one~~ *the reader* the where, when and why of the work. In
the last chapter, Shelley's love-life and death are
told about as taken from different resources.

Do not number the begining page of a chapter

CHAPTER II

HISTORY OF THE SHELLEYS

In order to better acquaint the reader with the actual person of Percy Bysshe Shelley, it would be wise to trace his ancestry and attempt to see if hereditary traits may have made him the way he was.

The pedigree of Shelley was first made public from the books of the College of Arms, in 1880; it began with the paternal line with Henry Shelley of Worminghurst in Sussex. More intense research traced the history of the poet to an ambassador to Spain in 1205, Sir Thomas. There is also tradition that the Shelleys came over with the Conqueror. John Shelley in 1415 married Beatrix Hawkwood, whose mother was the daughter of the Duke of Milan.

It seems that Shelley's relatives gave instances of
support of a cause which was in view. John Shelley's
great uncle was beheaded for attempting to set up
King Richard II. Another of the Shelleys was execu- *t*
ted for a conspiracy against Queen Elizabeth in favor
of Mary Queen of Scots. A synonymous note pertain-
ing to one of Shelley's relatives is that Thomas
Shelley in 1567 was "removed" from New College,
Oxford, for refusing to attend divine service. The
man considered the most Shelleyan in our sense was
l.c. a young Captain who served at Boulogne in 1545 under
the command of the poet Henry Howard, Earl of
Surrey. Because of his early and untimely death he
never received a reward justly due him but the Earl
wrote of him before he was notified of his death that
he promised more of that man, his truth and honesty,
than of any man he knew. The marriage of John
Shelley and Helen Bysshe brought the addition of Fen
Place to the Shelleys and also a name the poet was to
bear. In the beginning of the eighteenth century,

Edward Bysshe published a book The Art of English Poetry. Timothy Shelley, the third son of John and Helen, went to North America where there were other Shelleys. He became a merchant, married and has three sons John, Bysshe and Piercy. Bysshe, here, is sometimes referred to as Shelley's American grandfather. Bysshe was a favorite of his grandparents because of his good looks and manners; he later became well educated. He married three times and of the combined efforts of these women, Bysshe had many children. He gave John Shelley the name and arms of Sidney which formerly belonged to his last wife. Timothy, Bysshe's son by his first wife, went to Oxford where he received his B. A. and M. A. Timothy was a member of Parliament and a Whig Aristocrat and a fighter for parliamentary reform. He married Elizabeth Pilfolds and they resided at Field Place, Warnham. Shelley was to grow up at Field Place among the beautiful trees and always hold pleasant memories of it.

had

What is your source of information in this chapter?

You have condensed Shelley's ancestry so drastically that the relationship between the poet and the ancestors is not clear

Sp

CHAPTER III

SHELLEY'S EDUCATION

Shelley's education started when he was six years old. At this time his father sent him to Warham to learn Latin from the curate, Evan Edwards. During school holidays Shelley's father, Timothy, read the classics and other good books with him in the full hopes of "making him a good and gentlemanly scholar."[2] He became a good scholar but it was the gentlemanly scholar which Timothy Shelley really wanted to see. One such as William Pitt who Mr. Shelley said could overawe the House with a single Latin quotation.[3]

tr/lc

---

[2] Shelley, Edmund Blunden, New York: The Viking Press, 1947, p. 16.

[3] Ibid., p. 17.

The author of the book comes before the book's title

Shelley next attended Sion House Academy, whose buildings were in a declining state. The environment was not too good for a poet's education as may be inferred from its description in the last stanza of Thompson's "Castle of Indolence."

Even so through Brentford town, a town of mud,
An herd of bristly swine is pricked along.[4]

But this lack of beauty didn't detract from the fact that--Latin, Greek, French, writing, arithmetic, geography and the elements of astronomy were all capably taught under the direction of the master, Dr. Greenlaw.

It was conventional at Sion House that new boys were picked on for menial chores or as we say today, initiated or hazed. And Shelley turned out to be a perfect target because of his actions and his beauty. This place was a far cry from his beloved Field Place where he was brought up and the only enjoyment he had was his reading of books from the circulating library. Shelley was fascinated by tales of vampires,

---

[4]Ibid., p. 22.

headless horsemen and the like. But outside the
ecstasy of books Shelley was still seemingly perse-
cuted by the other school boys and he wrote:

> "I will be wise, and just, and free, and mild,
> if in me lies such power, for I grow weary
> to behold the selfish and the strong still tyrannize
> without reproach or check. "[5]

So it seems that since Shelley cannot physically beat
his opponents he will do it mentally.

There seems to be some controversy in my
reference books as to which school he was at, Sion
House or Eaton, but both describe about the same
thing under a different title. In The Winged Horse by
Auslander it is suggested that at Eaton fights were
frequent and that "Mad Shelley," as he was called,
was quite frequently taunted and pelted with mud.

As may have been depicted, Shelley's genius did
not escape everyone at Eaton. Master Keate saw
something in him. It was the fact that Shelley's
Latin prose usually included metrical sentences,
which he didn't even intend to put there, and so the
master applied to him a line from Ovid: Et quod

----

[5]Ibid., p. 24.

tentabam dicere versus erat. ("And what I tried to say fell into verse.")

It was mentioned before how Shelley would have to use his brains against the brawn of the other boys. He did it by forming what might be called an anti-fagging party. He complained to the teachers but was ignored and this last rebellious attempt resulted in his expulsion. It seems his party was against the whole system and it could not be tolerated. At this point I would like to bring in a personal opinion and say that here is a point of distaste concerning Shelley because he couldn't take it even though he acted valiantly in the direction he thought right.

avoid direct refer- ences to your- self.

Turning from Shelley's leisure hours to his classwork we find that he entered Eaton with a sound training in the classics and he was to depart with command of them. Eaton had what might be called a theoretical educational system which worked. Little was demanded of the boys but very much was expected and so they were left on their own. A Prime

Eton

sp

Minister of England once said: Whatever may be the
success in after life, whatever gratification or am-
bition may be realized, whatever triumphs may be
achieved, no one is ever again so great a man as
when he was a sixth form boy at Eaton.[6] Shelley
reached the sixth form.

You must use quotation marks whenever you use another's words

Sp.

Returning to Shelley's dislike of things at Eaton
his friend, Peacock, once said, "Shelley often spoke
to me of Eaton, and of the persecutions he had en-
dured from the older boys, with a feeling of abhor-
rence which I never heard him express in an equal
degree in relation to any other subject." Mr. Peacock later relates that Shelley said he was expelled
because he struck a penknife into the hand of one of
his young tyrants and pinned the knife to his desk;
Peacock also relates that Shelley's imagination often
presented events to him as they might have been, not
as they were. It was also suggested that others
would have remembered this incident if it were true.

Foot- note number?

---

[6] Ibid. p. 28.

[7] Ibid., p. 43.

Leigh Hunt gives his opinion that Shelley's reason for leaving prematurely was: "his unconventional spirit, penetrating, sincere, and demanding the justice of things was found to be inconvenient."[8] Evidence is also lacking to prove another tale concerning Shelley. This one was that during a rat hunt Shelley caught one of incredible age and size and identified him as the Founder. Another is that Shelley, by means of a mirror and gunpowder, blew up a forest.

Thus, it has been seen that Shelley probably didn't hold too much love for his old alma mater and he hoped things would be different at Oxford. He was sent to University College because his father had been at that college. One of Mr. Shelley's old friends now owned a printing shop and Mr. Shelley asked him to print some of his son's fancies.

Two months after Shelley signed the admission, he met his roommate, Thomas Jefferson Hogg. Hogg was to later write an incomplete, egotistical point of

---

[8] Ibid., p. 44.

view biography of Shelley. In this biography he tells of the first time he sees their room and describes it thusly: "Books, boots, papers, shoes, philosophical instruments, clothes, pistols, linen, crockery, ammunition, and phials innumerable, with money, stockings, prints, crucibles, bags and boxes, were scattered on the floor and in every place.... An electrical machine, an air-pump, the galvanic trough, a solar microscope, and large glass jars and receivers were conspicuous amidst the mass."[9]

"Oxford," Robert Southey wrote, "is a school for divinity, and nothing else."[10] Shelley, though, had learned logic. A short specimen of his logic was a manuscript, written within sight of the Chapel of University College, called The Necessity of Atheism. It amounted to saying that neither reason nor testimony is adequate to establish the existence of a diety, and that nothing short of a personal individual

---

[9] Ibid., p. 50.

[10] Ibid., p. 52.

self-revelation of the deity would be sufficient. [11]
This work was printed because of Shelley's influence
with the owner of a printing press. With the help of
Hogg these two men thought they had prepared an
unanswerable argument against the accepted notion
of God, or at least one which should stir up some
powerful reasoner for it. The postulate of the work
was: "The senses are the source of all knowledge to
the mind. "[12] For this manuscript Shelley was expelled from the school; when Hogg came to his de-
fense, he also was expelled. A point of interest here
might be that Shelley sent copies to the Bishop and
important men in the community. Thus, Shelley's
college career was cut painfully short.

_____

Which
edition?

[11]"Shelley", Encyclopaedia Britannica, vol. 20,
pp. 483-488.

[12]Ibid., p. 55.

CHAPTER IV

BACKGROUND FOR SHELLEY'S WORKS

At this time Shelley, against his philosophy,
married Harriet Westbrook. He also became enthus-
iastic and went to Ireland to work for Catholic
Emancipation. He wrote "Address to the Irish
People" which did not immediately succeed. Shelley
had decided on immediate remodeling of the world.[13]
He had written poems before. But now a desire to be
a hero swept him into a more ambitious effort. This
was a fervid tale of a dream in which he told how

> The iron rod of penury still compels
> Her wretched slave to bow the knee to wealth,

and how

> All things are sold: The very light of heaven
> Is venal.... Even love is sold.[14]

---

[13]Stephens, Beck, *and* Snow, *English Poets*, American Book Company, 1934, p. 411. *where published?*

[14]*The Winged Horse*, New York: Doubleday,
Doran and Company, 1927, p. 269. *author?*

May it be added here, that at this time Shelley was
receiving absolutely no money from his very rich
father. <u>Queen</u> <u>Mab</u> was dedicated to his wife,
Harriet; with the cry:

> ---thou wert my purer mind;
> Thou wert the inspiration of my song;
> Thine are these early wilding flowers
> Thou garlanded by me. [15]

<u>Queen</u> <u>Mab</u> was not thought to be all very good poetry,
but it has been described as strange, breathless, and
intense. After writing this poem, which Shelley
showed only to his friends, he and his wife returned
to England and Shelley now wanted to write more than
ever. In England his wife, Harriet, committed suicide and Shelley later married Mary Godwin. In
1818 he and his new wife Mary went to Italy to live
out their days. His first poem written in Italy was
<u>Alastor</u> where he set aside his political ideas to
write of the search for an ideal love. [16] This was a

Since there is an intervening footnote (The Winged Horse) you should have used loc. cit. instead of ibid.

---

[15]<u>Ibid</u>., p. 269.

[16]Stephens, Beck, Snow, (ibid.,) p. 413.

much better poem than Queen Mab. The story of
Alastor is that of a "youth of uncorrupted feelings
and adventurous genius" who goes searching for a
vision -- a woman -- of divine beauty. [17] Shelley was
very impressed with a girl with a pretty face.

The Revolt of Islam was his next poem. In this
work he talks as a poet-prophet in order to kindle or
start a virtuous enthusiasm for those doctrines of
liberty and justice, that faith and hope in something
good, which neither violence nor misrepresentation,
nor prejudice, can ever wholly extinguished.) ←

This is plagiarism. You may not use another writer's words without using quotation marks and giving the original writer credit with a footnote.

Stanzas Written in Dejection, Near Naples was
written after his daughter, Clara, and then his son,
William, died. In this poem his wish for death is not
long in coming, whether he meant it or not.

Prometheus Unbound, Shelley represents in
Prometheus the passion of humanity, or the aspiring
human mind, defying Jupiter, that despotic authority
which keeps men in chains. [18] Shelly gets his point,

---

[17]Auslander, The Winged Horse, New York:
Doubleday, Doran and Company, 1927, p. 273.

[18]Auslander, op. cit., p. 275.

that mind of man is joined in wedlock to his highest
and holiest aspirations, and universal love, by having
the Spirit, Asia, rescue Prometheus, dethrone Jupiter, and kill Tyranny. It was deduced by this author
that this poem combined Shelley's thoughts of man's
search for true liberties and true love.

Upon Keats' death, Shelley wrote one of the
greatest elegies in the language, the Adonais:

> See on the silken fringe of his fair eyes
> A tear some Dream has loosened from his brain!
> Lost angel of a ruined Paradise![19]

In 1820 Shelley produced a tragedy whose five
acts were founded on an actual account of the horrors
which ended with the fall of the House of Cenci at
Rome in 1599. This tragedy was called, The Cenci;
it was the only time he touched men and women of
flesh and blood in passionate action. He didn't think
much of it and once remarked that he only tried it
because he wanted to see if he could describe passions he had never felt.[20]

---

[19]Ibid., p. 276.

[20]Ibid.

A description of Shelley, that described his
reaching poetic ecstasy in his next few poems, was
given by Auslander as being: "Don't worry about his
ideas, he had none of any importance. He was just a
maker of deliciously beautiful music." This, although a fairly good description, is not wholly true.
He had his ideas, he hated tyranny, loved the glory
of freedom, and the beauty of tenderness and toler-
ance. After Shelley's death a poem was found ex-
pressing his protest against injustice.

A Dirge

Rough wind, that moanest loud
  Grief too sad for song;
Wild wind, when sullen cloud
  Knells all the night long;
Sad storms, whose tears are vain,
  Bare woods whose branches strain,
Deep caves and dreary main, --
  Wail, for the world's wrong.

This author thinks this poem to be very appealing.

Avoid direct refer- ences to your- self.

Although Shelley didn't like didactic poetry this poem
may be placed in that category because of its moral.

Shelley's yearning for freedom is plainly ex-
ressed in the first lines of Ode to the West Wind.

> O wild West Wind, thou breath of Autumn's being,
> Thou, from whose unseen presence the leaves dead
> Are driven, like ghosts from an enchanter fleeing,

These lines were followed most strongly by the ending:

> Scatter, as from an unextinguished hearth,
> Ashes and sparks, my words among mankind!
> Be through my lips to <u>unawakened</u> earth
> The trumpet of a phophecy! O Wind,
> If Winter comes, can Spring be far behind?

Thus it has been seen that through the beauty of his poetry Shelley fired up the people, urging them to a higher and purer endeavor. [21]

---

[21] Ibid., p. 280.

CHAPTER V

SIDELIGHTS ON SHELLEY

This author believes that one of the greatest

Do not make a direct reference to yourself

benefits of doing a paper such as this is to discover

the revealing, hidden facts of a person which one

may use at his discretion. Some of the sidelights

learned concerning Shelley were indeed interesting.

Use past tense

One was that Shelley believed in the philosophy

of free love and that one didn't have to marry. He

carried on, it was believed, some of this free love

with his cousin, Harriet Grove, then married Harriet

Westbrook. While having a little trouble with his

wife he went to see his good friend Godwin who also

believed with Shelley in the philosophy of free love.

Well, Godwin had a daughter to whom Godwin didn't

think this philosophy applied but to whom it was

applied by Shelley. He married her. Later it was
reported that Harriet Westbrook Shelley had committed suicide, a fate from which Shelley had origin-
ally saved her. So it may be seen that Shelley was
human and interesting.

Another interesting point pertains to Shelley's
death. While living happily with his wife, Mary, in
Italy he was visited by his good friend Leigh Hunt
who was at Leghorn. Shelley went in his boat, Ariel,
to bring him home. On the way home the ship cap-
sized and all were killed. Two weeks later, his
body was found on the beach. It was identified by the
books in his pockets, Sophocles and an unfinished
page of Keats. A story since then has gone around
that when the Ariel was salvaged it showed signs of
being rammed. Also, years later an old fisherman
on his death bed said he and his friends rammed the
Ariel with their fishing boat in hopes of robbing some
money thought to be aboard.

There is also a story that Trelawney and Byron
came back to the beach to burn the hastily buried
body that while Shelley was burning, his heart

defied the flames, Trelawney grabbed it and badly
burnt his hand. Byron turned and swam fiercely
away. Shelley's ashes were put in Protestant Ceme-
tary at Rome on December 7, 1822, near the grave of
Keats. So ended the life of a great English poet.

CHAPTER VI

CONCLUSION

It has been seen that Percy Bysshe Shelley led a nearly full and interesting life. His poetry will live forever and his person will also be admired for a long time. For one who was adverse to didactic poetry he had morals, even if they were different. *avoid direct refer-ences to your-self* This author shall always think of Shelley as energetic. He went to Ireland to speak on independence, he left England to go to Italy to write, he wrote constantly, he wrote well. He made up for his lack of physical prowess by being extremely smart, to the point where he developed his own philosophies. It is hard not to admit that Shelley was an idealist although he may have denied it.

Tracing the life of Shelley has been educational. From the history of the Shelleys, through his educa- *Spl.* tion and works, to his death gives one a greater scope of how things were at those times. This paper has been fully enjoyable and educational. To end the story, a descriptive quote from Auslander's <u>Winged</u>

<u>Horse</u> is appropriate, especially to Shelley.

> Higher still and higher
> From the earth thou springest
> Like a cloud of fire:
> The blue deep thou wingest,
> And singing still dust soar, and soaring ever
> singest.[22]

---

[22]Auslander, <u>The Winged Horse</u>, New York: Doubleday, Doran and Company, 1927.

BIBLIOGRAPHY

Auslander, Joseph and Hill, Frank, <u>The Winged Horse</u>. New York: Doubleday, Doran and Company, 1927. 452 pp.

Blunden, Edmund, <u>Shelley</u>, New York: The Viking Press, 1947. 378 pp.

Maurois, Andre, <u>Ariel</u>, New York: D. Appleton and Company, 1924. 336 pp.

"Shelley, Percy," Encyclopedia <u>Americana</u>, 1961 ed., vol. 22, pp. 688-691.

"Shelley, Percy," Encyclopaedia <u>Britannica</u>, 1956 ed., vol. 20, pp. 483-488.

Stephens, J., Beck, E., Snow, R., <u>English Poets</u>, New York: American Book Company, 1933. 1164 pp.

INDEX